D1116661

AMELIA EARHART

LEGENDARY AVIATOR

SPECIAL LIVES IN HISTORY THAT BECOME

Signature LIVES

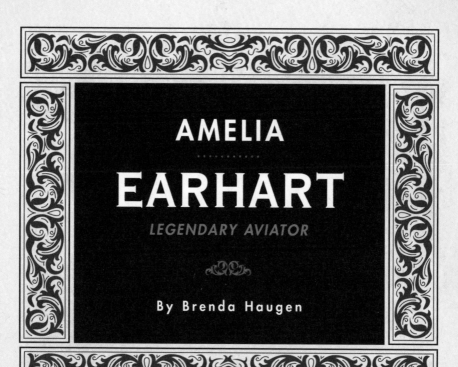

AMELIA
EARHART
LEGENDARY AVIATOR

By Brenda Haugen

Content Adviser: Michele Cervone,
Amelia Earhart Society of Researchers,
Clifton, New Jersey

Reading Adviser: Rosemary G. Palmer, Ph.D.,
Department of Literacy, College of Education,
Boise State University

COMPASS POINT BOOKS MINNEAPOLIS, MINNESOTA

Compass Point Books
3109 West 50th Street, #115
Minneapolis, MN 55410

Visit Compass Point Books on the Internet at *www.compasspointbooks.com*
or e-mail your request to *custserv@compasspointbooks.com*

Editor: Sue Vander Hook
Page Production: Blue Tricycle
Photo Researchers: Abbey Fitzgerald and Marcie C. Spence
Cartographer: XNR Productions, Inc.
Library Consultant: Kathleen Baxter

Art Director: Jaime Martens
Creative Director: Keith Griffin
Editorial Director: Carol Jones
Managing Editor: Catherine Neitge

In memory of Scotti Greenan, who helped me understand
the joy and freedom of flying. *BLH*

Library of Congress Cataloging-in-Publication Data
Haugen, Brenda
  Amelia Earhart: legendary aviator / by Brenda Haugen
  p. cm—(Signature lives)
  Includes bibliographical references and index.
ISBN-13: 978-0-7565-1880-6 (hardcover)
ISBN-10: 0-7565-1880-6 (hardcover)
ISBN-13: 978-0-7565-1984-1 (paperback)
ISBN-10: 0-7565-1984-5 (paperback)
1. Earhart, Amelia, 1879–1937—Juvenile literature. 2. Air pilots—United
States—Biography—Juvenile literature. 3. Women air pilots—United
States—Biography—Juvenile literature. I. Title.
  TL540.E3H38 2006
  629.13092—dc22   2006003826

Signature Lives

MODERN AMERICA

Starting in the late 19th century, advancements in all areas of human activity transformed the world into a new and modern place. Inventions prompted rapid shifts in lifestyle, and scientific discoveries began to alter the way humanity viewed itself. Beginning with World War I, warfare took place on a global scale, and ideas such as nationalism and communism showed that countries were taking a larger view of their place in the world. The combination of all these changes continues to produce what we know as the modern world.

Table of Contents

1 HISTORIC FLIGHT

❦

Rain and fog made it impossible for the pilot of the *Friendship* to spot land. It was June 18, 1928, and the three people onboard the airplane were weary from flying over the Atlantic Ocean for more than 20 hours. When the rain finally subsided and the fog lifted, the three simultaneously shouted, "Land!" They were off the coast of Wales on the west side of Great Britain.

Since the plane was rigged with pontoons for a water landing, pilot Wilmer "Bill" Stultz landed on the water at Burry Port. Co-pilot Louis "Slim" Gordon and passenger Amelia Earhart were relieved at the safe landing. The logbook read, "20 hrs. 40 mins. out of Trepassey *Friendship* down safely in harbor of Burry Port, Wales."

At first, local townspeople weren't very interested

Co-pilot Louis "Slim" Gordon (left), passenger Amelia Earhart, and pilot Wilmer "Bill" Stultz were the crew of the Friendship *on the 1928 transatlantic flight.*

The Atlantic Ocean got its name from the ancient Romans, who named the great body of water after the Atlas Mountains that rise at the western end of the Mediterranean Sea. The Atlantic Ocean covers 17 percent of Earth's total surface and makes up more than one-fourth of the planet's total ocean area. It is bordered by North America and South America on the west and Europe and Africa on the east. At its widest point, the ocean spans about 5,500 miles (8,800 kilometers). At its narrowest point, the ocean narrows to about 1,800 miles (2,880 km). The Pacific is the only ocean larger than the Atlantic.

in the plane or its occupants. It was almost an hour before a local sheriff rowed a small boat out to the Fokker F7 airplane to talk to the crew. People in England, Scotland, and Ireland knew about the *Friendship*, however, and had been watching for it to arrive. But Stultz had missed his Southampton, England, target and ended up in Wales. In spite of where they landed, this was a historic journey. Amelia Earhart had just become the first woman in history to make a transatlantic flight. She had flown from Trepassey, Newfoundland, in Canada, to Wales.

Residents of Burry Port soon realized how important this woman was. When Earhart stepped ashore, nearly the entire population of the small town greeted her. Members of the overeager crowd tried to grab her clothes, shake her hand, and get her autograph. A protective circle, including the police and a reporter from *The New York Times*, formed around Earhart and helped her reach the nearest building.

"In the enthusiasm of their greeting those hospitable people nearly tore our clothes off," Earhart recalled.

Although shocked by the attention, Earhart took

The crowd swarmed Amelia Earhart after her transatlantic flight in June 1928.

Earhart's visit to London in June 1928 brought cheers and celebration from British children.

it all in stride. She accepted her new fame gracefully, repeatedly giving all the credit to Stultz and Gordon.

Earhart didn't see her transatlantic journey as much of a personal accomplishment. After all, she had merely served as a passenger on the flight. But she realized the publicity would be important in advancing airplanes as a means of transportation. When asked if she was excited about her historic journey, she seemed surprised and saw little reason for celebration. She said:

> *Excited? No. ... It was a grand experience but all I did was lie on my tummy and take pictures of the clouds. We didn't see much of the ocean. Stultz did all the flying—had to. I was just baggage, like a sack of potatoes.*

She had wanted to pilot the plane, at least for a little while, but wasn't allowed to do so. That task had been left to Stultz, one of the best pilots of his day. Earhart's friend, Captain Hilton H. Railey, who had arranged for her to make the flight, insisted that what she had done was important, even if she hadn't been at the controls. Earhart smiled and said, "Oh, well, maybe some day I'll try it alone."

In fact, Earhart would do just that and would go on to achieve many firsts in aviation. She always hoped the work she did would inspire others—particularly women—to follow their dreams, whatever those dreams might be. ✥

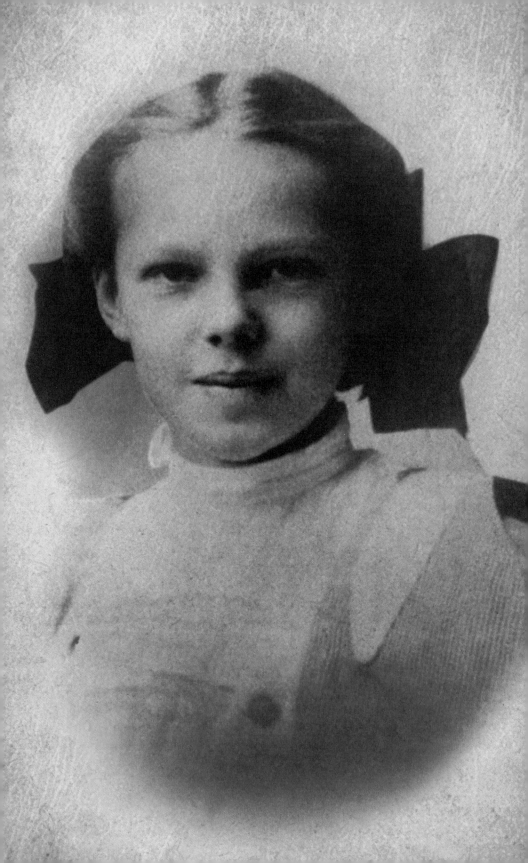

Chapter 2 Happy Beginning

Amelia Mary Earhart was born on July 24, 1897. Her parents, Amy Otis Earhart and Edwin Stanton Earhart, welcomed her into the world at 11:30 P.M. in Atchison, Kansas, at the home of Amy's parents. They didn't take any chances with this birth, since the couple had suffered the tragic loss of their first child just a year before. When Amy was pregnant, a cable car in which she was traveling had been involved in an accident. She went into premature labor, and their first baby girl didn't survive.

Amelia's parents loved each other and were happy together, even though they lived on a tight budget. Amy had been raised in a well-to-do home, but Edwin was not a rich man. His private law practice wasn't successful, and money was always an issue. When

Amelia Earhart (1897–1939) at the age of 7

a tax collector showed up at their door one day, Amy realized her husband had been irresponsible. Edwin, who fancied himself an inventor, had wasted their money trying to get a patent on an invention. Unfortunately, someone else had invented the same thing two years earlier.

On December 29, 1899, Amy and Edwin welcomed the birth of another daughter—Grace Muriel. They called her Muriel. The Earhart family was now complete. Growing up, Amelia and Muriel never knew about their father's money problems. They loved him because he always seemed to find time to play and read with them. In 1904, Edwin managed to take his family to the World's Fair in St. Louis, Missouri. The roller coaster ride there appealed to Amelia so much that when they got back to Kansas, she decided to build her own, with the help of Muriel and their uncle Carl Otis.

The homemade roller coaster

The St. Louis World's Fair included pools, gardens, and large exhibition halls.

consisted of a wooden box that flew across wood planks greased with lard. Seven-year-old Amelia took the first ride, which turned out to be her last. The box and Amelia crashed, and she ended up with a bruised lip and a torn dress. Undeterred, she exclaimed, "Oh, Pidge (her sister's nickname), it's just like flying." Amelia made plans to extend the track and straighten the frame, but her mother quickly brought the adventure to an end. After seeing Amelia's injury, Amy insisted the roller coaster be torn down.

Amy was concerned about her children, but she wasn't an overprotective mother. She let her girls be who they wanted to be. When her daughters chose activities considered boyish, like walking on stilts, she allowed them the freedom to try. Although Amelia was a bit of a tomboy, her mother never attempted to make her change. She even let her daughters dress in special-made dark blue flannel clothes called bloomers that were similar to gym clothes. The outfits were an embarrassment to the girls' grandmother. Amelia would later admit:

Amelia (right) with her dog, toy sled, and sister, Muriel

We wore them Saturdays to play in and though we felt terribly "free and athletic," we also felt somewhat as outcasts among

*the little girls who fluttered about us in
their skirts.*

When not playing, Amelia often spent her time
reading. Some stories she had read so many times
that she knew them by heart. She also liked to write
poetry, which sometimes came from her dreams
about flying.

> *I watch the birds flying all day long
> And I want to fly too.
> Don't they look down sometimes, I wonder,
> And wish they were me
> When I'm going to the circus with
>   my daddy?*

When Amelia was 8, her father closed his failing
law office and took a job with the Rock Island Railroad in Des Moines, Iowa. Until their parents found
a house and got settled, Amelia and Muriel lived with
their grandparents in Atchison. The girls expected to
stay with them for about two months, but that turned
into nearly a year. They attended a private school in
the area. Though they missed their parents, Amelia
and Muriel loved being around their grandparents
and cousins. Amelia also liked their library, which
had many more books than her parents' collection.

At Christmastime, Amy and Edwin returned to
Atchison to spend the holiday with their family. They

brought gifts for their daughters, including boys' sleds—just what the girls wanted. Unlike proper girls' sleds of the day, which young ladies sat upon, boys' sleds allowed riders to flop down on their bellies. Grandmother Otis was horrified. To add to her displeasure, the girls also received real rifles from their father. These would replace their BB guns. Edwin assured his mother-in-law that the girls were well-trained in the care and responsibility of a gun, though that did little to make her happy.

After Amy and Edwin got settled in Des Moines, they sent for their daughters. Amy hired a widow named Florence Gardiner to serve as the girls' governess and teacher. She taught them French, reading, and sewing. However, Gardiner didn't fit in with the Earhart family, and they parted ways. Amelia and Muriel then attended public school.

The summer Amelia turned 10, her family went to the Iowa State Fair. There Amelia saw an airplane for the first time. It had been four years since Wilbur and Orville Wright had made their historic flight in an airplane that was heav-

The Iowa State Fair began in 1854 to display the Midwest's agricultural resources such as corn, wheat, and cattle. As more pioneers ventured westward and Iowa's population grew, so did the fair and its attractions. By 1896, the fair was attracting crowds with spectacular events like locomotive collisions. By 1911, eight years after Wilbur and Orville Wright made their historic flight, the fair offered daredevil mid-air stunts in the latest flying machines, as airplanes were sometimes called.

ier than air at Kitty Hawk, North Carolina. People were interested in these flying machines, as they were sometimes called. But the plane Amelia saw was made of rusty wire and wood, and she wasn't very impressed. It would be another eight years before she would see another airplane and become interested in flying.

Things were changing and improving financially for the Earharts. Amelia's father was promoted at work, and his salary nearly doubled. Because he now had an important position with the Rock Island Railroad, Edwin and his family could travel in a private railroad car. Edwin often took his family on long business trips, even if the girls had to miss school. He believed that seeing the world was an important learning experience.

With Edwin's bump in salary, the Earharts were able to move into a bigger house and hire a cook and a maid. In the summertime, they vacationed in Minnesota, where Amelia especially enjoyed riding horses.

However, with all that was going right for the Earharts, one thing was going terribly wrong. Edwin had developed a drinking problem, and life for the Earhart family would never be the same. ❧

3 TURBULENT TIMES

੨๛

No one is sure when Edwin's problem with alcohol began, but it was obvious how it started. Every night after work, he socialized with co-workers and others who went to a bar before going home to their families. Soon Edwin found himself unable to turn away from alcohol, and both his family life and career suffered. When Edwin drank, he turned into someone his daughters no longer recognized. Gone was the man who loved to read to them and play games. He became an angry man, and his daughters learned to avoid him when he was drunk. Amelia learned a lesson from her father's addiction and promised herself she would never drink alcohol.

When Edwin's drinking began to affect his work, his boss insisted he check into a hospital. After a monthlong hospital stay, Edwin seemed to be his old self again. His family was thrilled. However, within a few days, he was drinking again, and he lost his job permanently. Amy's parents had always doubted that Edwin could provide for their daughter, and now that was coming true. Before her death, Amy's mother placed her daughter's inheritance in a trust for 20 years, or until Edwin's death, whichever came first. She didn't want Edwin to squander all the money.

Edwin felt insulted, which caused him to drink more. His reputation as an alcoholic quickly made its way through the railroad industry, and he found it difficult to get another job doing what he had done in the past. Finally, he took a position as a clerk with the Great Northern Railway freight office in St. Paul, Minnesota. His salary was much lower than he was used to earning, but at least it was a job.

The Earharts packed up their belongings and traveled to St. Paul by railroad coach, the inexpensive seats. Gone were the days of traveling in a private railway car. Amelia and Muriel saw their mother quietly crying, but they were excited about getting a fresh start. In their new

The Great Northern Railway was created in 1889 by combining several railroads in Minnesota. Eventually, its tracks stretched from Minnesota through North Dakota, Montana, Idaho, and Washington. In 1970, the Great Northern Railway merged with several other railroad companies to form the Burlington Northern Railroad, which still operates today.

town, the family rented a house, but the cost of rent and heat ate up nearly all of Edwin's paycheck.

Amelia attended Central High School and enjoyed her classes, particularly Latin and physics. But her family wouldn't stay long in St. Paul. In the spring, Edwin was offered a better job with the Burlington Railroad in Springfield, Missouri, so the family moved again. Unfortunately, when they got to Springfield, Edwin discovered the job no longer existed. The man whom Edwin was hired to replace had changed

Amelia's father worked for the Great Northern Railway in St. Paul, Minnesota.

his mind and decided to keep working. Edwin took a temporary job while he continued to search for permanent employment.

Amy decided that her daughters needed a more stable home, so she took them with her to Chicago to stay with their friends, the Shedds. The Earharts had once given the Shedds a place to stay, and now the Shedds returned the favor. Amy and the girls would return to Springfield when Edwin had a steady job and a permanent residence.

When Edwin's job search proved unsuccessful, he decided to go to Kansas City, Missouri, and open up another law office. His wife and daughters stayed in Chicago while he got settled. Not wanting to wear out their welcome with the Shedds, Amy found a small apartment where she and the girls could live.

Amelia attended Hyde Park High School in Chicago, but she was soon disappointed with the lack of discipline. In her English class in particular, students were unruly and disrespectful. After two weeks of classes, Amelia asked for permission to spend her English period in the library. Her request was approved, but it didn't make her very popular with other students. When Amelia graduated in 1916, the caption under her senior picture read, "The girl in brown who walks alone." Since Amelia felt no special bond with her school, she decided to skip the graduation ceremony.

After Amelia graduated, the Earhart women joined Edwin in a small house in Kansas City. Amy realized she would need money to send her daughters to college, so she went to court to have her mother's will changed so she could receive her inheritance. Although her brother had spent some of her inheritance, about $40,000 still remained. The court granted her request, and Amy became, once again, a woman of considerable wealth for the time. ✍

Amelia attended Hyde Park High School in Chicago, Illinois.

4 HER PATH IN LIFE

❦

With her inheritance money, Amy sent her daughters to college. Although Amelia wasn't sure what she wanted to do with her life, she went to college at Ogontz School in Rydal, Pennsylvania, in the fall of 1916. She attracted friends, joined a sorority, served as vice president of her class, leader of the glee club, secretary of the school's Red Cross chapter, and secretary and treasurer of a religious group called the Christian Endeavor.

In 1917, Earhart traveled to Toronto, Canada, to visit Muriel, who was attending St. Margaret's College. Walking along a street one day, Earhart saw firsthand the results of World War I, which had been raging for three years. Four men were on crutches; each had lost a leg during the fighting. Earhart wanted to help,

Earhart worked at the Spadina Military Hospital in Toronto, Canada.

so she quit school and stayed in Canada. She completed a Red Cross first aid class and joined the Volunteer Aid Detachment. At Canada's Spadina Military Hospital, Earhart emptied bedpans, scrubbed floors, and completed whatever tasks needed to be done.

She worked from 7 A.M. to 7 P.M. with a two-hour afternoon break. When the director of nurses at the hospital found out Earhart had studied chemistry, she asked her to help in the pharmacy and kitchen. Earhart made it her mission to make the hospital's dull food more appetizing for the ailing veterans.

During her free time, Earhart went horseback riding with Muriel. On occasion, an officer with the British Royal Flying Corps joined the young women. He invited them to visit the airfield where he flew but couldn't offer them a plane ride because it was against military rules to allow civilians to fly. Earhart enjoyed being around planes and soon discovered her fascination with flight. She later wrote:

I hung around in spare time and absorbed all I could. I remember the sting of the

*snow on my face as it was blown back
from the propellers.*

At a Toronto fair, Earhart saw war aces giving stunt-flying demonstrations. As Earhart, her sister, and a friend stood in a clearing to get the best possible view, a pilot decided to give the crowd a thrill and began diving toward the young women. Earhart remembered:

He was bored. He had looped and rolled and spun and finished his little bag of tricks, and there was nothing left to do but watch the people on the ground running as he swooped close to them.

Earhart learned many things about flying by watching British Royal Flying Corps pilots at the Toronto airfield.

As the pilot swooped down, the others ran off in fear, but Earhart stood firm. She later recalled:

> *I remember the mingled fear and pleasure which surged over me as I watched that small plane at the top of its earthward swoop. ... I did not understand it at the time but I believe that little red airplane said something to me as it swished by.*

Masked doctors and nurses treated flu patients lying on cots and in outdoor tents during the flu epidemic of 1918.

That year, 1918, a deadly flu epidemic struck Toronto. Around the world, about 20 million people died from it. Though Earhart avoided the flu, she did become ill from working too hard in the pneumonia ward at the hospital where she volunteered. While

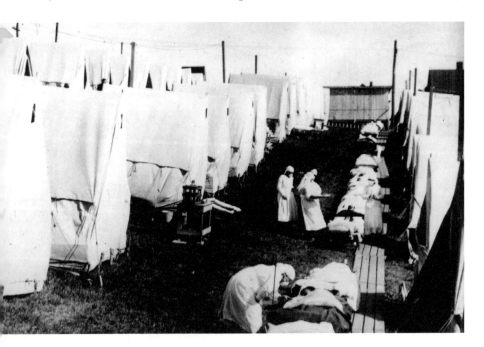

Amelia recovered, Muriel transferred to a school in Massachusetts. Later, Amelia joined her sister and shared her small Northampton apartment.

In Northampton, Earhart was still not on a career path. She took time to indulge her love of music, playing the piano and practicing the banjo. Always practical, she also took a five-week course in automobile mechanics, which taught her the basics of engines. That skill would later be very useful.

In the fall of 1919, Earhart believed she knew what she wanted to do with her life. She enrolled in the premed program at Columbia University in New York City. However, it didn't take long for her to realize she didn't want to be a practicing doctor. But she believed she might like a job in medical research.

By this time, Earhart's parents were on the West Coast and suggested she come to California to continue her education. Although she didn't want to go, Earhart realized her parents' marriage was in trouble, and she wanted to help. She made a deal with her sister. She would go to California and stay with their parents while Muriel finished college. When Muriel earned her degree, she would go to California while Amelia moved back East and resumed her life.

Muriel agreed, and Earhart headed to California. Although her father had stopped drinking, her parents were still facing financial woes. Earhart's mother had invested $22,000 in a mining operation in

Nevada. When the mine flooded, she lost her money and couldn't pay for Muriel's final year of college or for more college for Amelia.

Though Earhart was disappointed, she faced it with a good attitude and didn't become bitter. She was happy to see her father's health return and enjoyed spending time with him. Father and daughter especially enjoyed going to air circuses. These flying exhibitions, common in the early 1920s, included stunt flying and attempts at speed records. The goal of an air circus was to get the public interested in flying. In Earhart's case, it worked.

Edwin Earhart didn't think his daughter would choose a career as a pilot, but he wanted to satisfy her curiosity. He arranged a trial flight for her. Amelia remembered, "I am sure he thought one ride would be enough for me, and he might as well cure me promptly."

The field where Earhart's plane took off was vacant land on what is now Wilshire Boulevard in Los Angeles. The pilot was Frank

Barnstormers were the aerial daredevils of the 1920s. When World War I ended in 1918, many former military pilots looked for ways to make a living. Some of them purchased planes for as little as $200 and organized flying teams. Unannounced, a team would fly over a small town and land at a local farm (thus the word "barnstorming"). After making a deal with the farmer to use his fields as runways, the pilots would "buzz the village," or fly back over the town, to drop advertisements for airplane rides and daring aerial shows. Almost every business shut down so people could attend what was called an air circus.

Daredevil stunt flyer Ormer Locklear balanced in flight atop his airplane to entertain onlookers.

Hawks, who would one day become a famous aviator and break many speed records. A third person joined them, probably to protect Earhart, who later wrote:

> *I was a girl—a "nervous lady." I might jump out. There had to be somebody on hand to grab my ankle as I went over. It was no use to explain I had seen aeroplanes before and wasn't excitable.*

To Edwin's dismay, the flight failed to satisfy his daughter's desire to fly. In fact, Earhart now believed it was her destiny. When she told her parents, they didn't think she was serious. But she proved how serious she was by finding a pilot to give her lessons. ✍

5 PILOT AND TEACHER

Chapter

⋐⋐✕⋑⋑

By telling his daughter he couldn't afford flying lessons, Edwin hoped Amelia would give up thoughts of flying. But she wasn't deterred. Earhart found a job with a California telephone company and saved up money to pay for her own lessons. On January 3, 1921, Earhart had her first flying lesson.

Her instructor was a female pilot named Neta "Snooky" Snook. In the early 1920s, most pilots were veterans of World War I. Earhart was afraid she would feel intimidated taking lessons from one of these war aces, so she had searched for a female pilot. Earhart described Snooky:

> She dresses and talks like a man and can
> do everything around a plane that a man

Neta "Snooky" Snook was Earhart's first flight instructor.

can do. I'm lucky that she'll teach me, not only because she will give me lessons on credit, but because she is a top-notch flier and one of the first women to get a pilot's license in Canada.

Soon Earhart had cut her hair shorter and began dressing like other pilots. So she would look more experienced, she slept in her new leather flying jacket and rubbed airplane oil on it so it would look worn.

Neta Snook (1896–1991) had been flying for four years when she met Amelia Earhart in December 1920. She earned a living taking people on 15-minute airplane rides for $15 per flight and barnstorming as a stunt pilot. In 1922, Snook gave up flying to get married and have children. She didn't fly again until 1977 at the age of 81, when she piloted a replica of Charles Lindbergh's airplane, the Spirit of St. Louis. She lived to be 95 years old.

In those days, planes were unreliable, and a pilot had to be prepared to land almost anywhere. Engines often failed. Snook and Earhart once crashed into a cabbage patch. But Earhart was an eager student, and soon it was time for her to fly solo—all by herself.

In June 1921, Muriel arrived in California in time to watch her sister solo. Earhart took to the sky in a Model K Kinner Airster biplane. Pilots didn't need a license at that time, and Earhart wouldn't receive her pilot's license until 1923. She would be the 16th person to earn a license from the National Aeronautic Association in Washington, D.C.

On July 24, 1922, Earhart celebrated her 25th birthday by buying her first airplane. Her mother and Muriel helped her come up with the money to buy it from airplane designer William Kinner. Earhart named the bright yellow, two-seater biplane *Canary*. She worked out a deal with Kinner. She would let him use her plane for demonstrations in exchange for space to store it in his hangar.

Earhart stood by her first plane, a Kinner named Canary.

Amelia Earhart's photo as it appeared on her pilot's license, which she received in 1923.

Earhart wasted no time putting her flying skills to use. On October 22, 1922, she participated in an air circus at Rogers Air Field in Los Angeles. While her parents watched, she tried for an altitude record. Although the airplane had problems ascending, she didn't bring it down until she had climbed to 14,000 feet (4,200 m). Now Amelia Earhart had secured her first women's aviation record.

The record was cause for celebration, but it was clouded by strife at home. The move to the West Coast had not helped save her parents' marriage, and they finally divorced. Amelia, Muriel, and Amy decided to move to Boston, Massachusetts. Muriel traveled there by train, but Earhart wanted to fly there with her mother. Amy was reluctant, however, so Earhart sold her plane and bought a bright yellow Kissel sports car. Earhart drove her mother to their new home on one of the longest routes she could find, leisurely taking in the sights of national parks along the way. When they arrived, Muriel was there to greet them.

By 1925, Muriel was enjoying a career as a teacher, and she thought her sister would also enjoy that job. Earhart enrolled once again at Columbia University but didn't stay long enough to earn a degree. At Muriel's suggestion, Earhart took classes at Harvard University in Cambridge, Massachusetts, and received a teaching license. She spent several months teaching foreign students at the University of Massachusetts.

In 1925, Amelia Earhart attended Harvard University in Cambridge, Massachusetts.

Earhart's love of flying never waned, however.

She found out that airplane designer William Kinner had also moved to the East Coast and that he still owned a plane. When no paying customers were around, Kinner let Earhart fly. In return, Earhart demonstrated his plane for potential buyers and kept the engine in top condition. Male pilots quickly grew to respect Earhart. They appreciated her flying skills and her willingness to get her hands dirty while fixing an engine.

But Earhart still needed to make a living, and in August 1926, she responded to an advertisement for part-time English teachers at a school called the Denison House in Boston. She got the job, which required her to teach foreign students and sometimes help them in their personal lives. This appealed to Earhart, and she became friends with many of the students. She visited them in their homes, and they often shared meals together. In less than a year, Earhart was working as a full-time teacher and moved into an apartment above the school so she could be available whenever she was needed.

> During the two years that Earhart taught at the Denison House, she spent most of her weekends flying. Once she dropped flyers from her plane over Boston to advertise an event at the school.

Earhart was also busy with her social life. In Los Angeles, she had met Sam Chapman, and they had become engaged to be married. When Earhart moved

Amelia Earhart and Sam Chapman in California

to Boston, Chapman followed her. He made a good living and offered her a comfortable life. Although she cared deeply for him, Earhart realized after a while that she didn't want to settle down and be a stay-at-home wife. She broke off the engagement, but the two would always remain friends.

She never lost her interest in airplanes, however. As often as possible, she flew out of the Boston airport. It was only natural that her name would come up when a woman was being sought for a historic flight across the Atlantic Ocean. ✍

6 FIRST TRANSATLANTIC FLIGHT

❦

One April day in 1928, a student at Denison House brought Earhart a message. A man wanted to speak to her on the telephone. Earhart was bustling around making sure children went to class and teachers were ready to greet them. She told the youngster to say she was busy and didn't have time for a phone call.

When the child insisted the call was important, Earhart reluctantly picked up the phone. World War I Army Captain Hilton H. Railey was on the other end. He asked her if she would be interested "in doing something for aviation that might be hazardous."

At first, Earhart thought the call was a joke. However, she quickly realized he was serious. He explained that Amy Guest, a wealthy socialite, had purchased a plane called *Friendship* and planned

Amelia Earhart in Boston before her historic transatlantic flight in June 1928

Amy Guest decided not to fly across the Atlantic Ocean but insisted another woman take her place.

to become the first woman to fly across the Atlantic Ocean. However, her family's strong feelings against the dangerous adventure caused her to change her mind. Several women had attempted the flight before, and all had failed. Some had even lost their lives trying.

Guest insisted that another woman be chosen to take her place on what would be a historic journey. Railey was given the job of finding that woman. After asking around, Railey was told to call Denison House and ask for Amelia Earhart. Soon after the call, Earhart and Railey met.

Railey told Earhart about the plan for a transatlantic crossing. Earhart was excited about the opportunity to be aboard, but she wanted to pilot the plane, at least part of the way. He said that probably wouldn't happen. Even though she had her pilot's license, Earhart didn't know how to fly with instruments in a multi-motored aircraft, a skill that was necessary to fly over the ocean. Always ready for an adventure, Earhart agreed to go.

Railey set up a meeting with the people who would decide if Earhart was right for the job. Some of them would represent Amy Guest. New York publisher George Putnam would also be there. Always looking for new opportunities for best-selling books, he had joined the project when Guest first bought a plane and planned her transatlantic flight. Now he was interested in meeting the woman who might take Guest's place.

Hilton H. Railey asked Amelia Earhart to make a transatlantic flight.

Earhart traveled to New York City for the interview. The meeting went well, and Earhart returned to Boston. Two days later, she received a note and a formal agreement from Guest, who invited Earhart to join pilot Wilmer "Bill" Stultz, backup pilot Louis Gower, and mechanic Louis "Slim" Gordon on the transatlantic flight. Although Earhart wouldn't be paid for her part in the adventure, she was fine with that and happy to be part of it.

To keep her plans of the transatlantic flight quiet, Earhart steered clear of the airport where the *Friendship* was housed. She wrote:

I did not dare show myself around Boston airport where the ship [plane] was being worked on. ... To have been detected in the picture would have brought premature publicity and swamped all concerned with thrill writers and curiosity seekers.

While waiting for her adventure to begin, Earhart went on with her life as if nothing were out of the ordinary. She continued teaching and shared her transatlantic plans only with Sam Chapman and a co-worker. She gave Chapman the task of telling her mother and sister about her adventure, but only after she had flown out of Boston.

Earhart knew the journey across the Atlantic was dangerous and that there was a chance she wouldn't return. She left letters for her parents if her adventure failed. If she died, she wanted her mother to read these words: "Even though I have lost, the adventure was worth while. ... My life has really been very happy, and I didn't mind contemplating its end in the midst of it."

In a letter to her father, Earhart was positive and cheerful. "Hooray for the last grand adventure!" she wrote. "I wish I had won, but it was worthwhile, anyway. You know that I have no faith we'll meet anywhere again, but I wish we might."

In a longer letter to Muriel, Earhart explained why she didn't share her plans before leaving.

I haven't told you about the affair as I didn't want to worry mother, and she would suspect (she may now) if I told you. ... I couldn't stand the added strain of telling mother and you personally. If reporters talk to you, say you knew, if you like.

The *Friendship* was transformed for the transatlantic flight. It was painted orange and gold so it could be spotted more easily if it went down in the Atlantic Ocean. Pontoons replaced the usual wheels so the plane could land on water. Two large gas tanks were added, even though they took up much of the

Workmen put fuel in the tanks of the Friendship *aircraft a few days before takeoff.*

cabin space. The extra fuel would be necessary for such a long journey. A small table covered with navigation equipment was the only furniture inside the plane. The crew would have to sit on 5-gallon (19-liter) water cans.

By June 1928, the *Friendship* was ready for takeoff. However, the weather wasn't cooperating. When the sky was finally clear enough to fly, Stultz couldn't get the plane airborne. The aircraft was too heavy for liftoff. There weren't many options for lightening the load. All the fuel and equipment were

Earhart posed next to an airplane in Newfoundland, Canada, before her 1928 flight over the Atlantic Ocean.

necessary, and each crew member only had a few essentials. After three unsuccessful attempts to take off, the decision was finally made to leave Gower behind. The change in weight was enough, and the *Friendship* was in the air.

Newspaper reporters heard about the flight and quickly printed stories. They hounded the Earharts with questions, but since Chapman hadn't yet told them about the flight, they had few answers.

Meanwhile, Earhart was dealing with problems of her own in the plane. The latch for the cabin door broke off just before takeoff, and she had to hold the door shut. She and Gordon were nearly pulled out of the plane before Gordon was able to fix the latch with string.

From Boston, the *Friendship* flew to Halifax, Nova Scotia, in Canada, where it landed on the waters near shore. Grounded by fog, the crew got a hotel for the night, where reporters swarmed around them. The adventurers refueled the next morning and flew to Trepassey, Newfoundland, their last stop before crossing the Atlantic.

The group planned to leave Trepassey on June 5, but strong winds forced them to wait nearly two weeks. Waiting was difficult for all of them. While Earhart passed the time playing cards or reading, Stultz turned to alcohol. He was one of the best pilots in the world, but when he drank, he gave orders that didn't make sense and quickly reacted with anger. Earhart could have complained and had him replaced, but she remembered what a bad reputation had done to her father and didn't want that to happen to Stultz.

On June 16, the crew received word that they could expect good weather over the Atlantic for the next two days. However, on the morning of June 17, Stultz had passed out from drinking too much. Earhart and Gordon splashed cold water on him and made him drink coffee. Then they maneuvered him to the plane. By that time, Stultz had regained his senses enough to fly. The *Friendship* didn't take off on the first try. Earhart recalled:

> *I was crowded in the cabin with a stop watch in my hand to check the take-off time, and with my eyes glued on the air speed indicator as it slowly climbed. If it passed fifty miles an hour, chances were the* Friendship *could pull out and fly. Thirty—forty—the* Friendship *was trying again. A long pause, then the pointer went to fifty. Fifty, fifty-five—sixty. We were off at last.*

Earhart would later admit that this takeoff was the most dangerous part of the entire flight. The plane rocked as it cut through the water, and the salty spray caused both engines to sputter.

Aloft, the *Friendship* soon disappeared from spectators' views, only to show up a few minutes later circling back over Trepassey Harbor. Then they flew northeast, but predictions of good weather soon proved wrong. The crew was dealing with strong winds, heavy rain, and eventually snow. But they were able to weather the storm, and the plane again flew into fair skies.

Mabel Boll wanted to be the first woman to fly across the Atlantic Ocean, but Earhart beat her to it.

As the *Friendship* made its way across the Atlantic, word leaked out on both sides of the ocean that Earhart and her crew were attempting the crossing. Among the most eager to hear word of the flight was the crew of a airplane called the *Columbia*. Mabel Boll had planned to be the first woman to cross the Atlantic Ocean. In fact, Stultz had been interviewed as a potential pilot for Boll's flight. He never told her about his plans to fly the *Friendship*.

Meanwhile, the crew members onboard the *Friendship* weren't sure they would make it to England. With only an hour's worth of

Charles Lindbergh (1902–1974) had also accepted the challenge to fly solo nonstop across the Atlantic Ocean. He accomplished this historic feat on May 20–21, 1927, in his Ryan monoplane named the Spirit of St. Louis. Lindbergh was born in 1902 in Detroit, Michigan, and grew up near Little Falls, Minnesota. He started college at the University of Wisconsin but quit two years later to become a barnstormer, a pilot who performed stunts at fairs. He also served as a pilot for the U.S. Army.

fuel remaining, they weren't even sure where they were. Clouds obstructed their view, and their radio was dead. According to their calculations, they should have passed Ireland by this time. Indeed, they had passed the southern edge of the country, but they didn't see it because of heavy cloud cover.

The worried crew considered giving up, but then they spotted a ship. Since the *Friendship* was equipped for water landing, they could have landed and boarded the ship, but they all agreed to keep going. Their courage was rewarded by the sight of fishing boats, which meant that land had to be near. It had been nearly 20 hours and 40 minutes since they left Newfoundland. Earhart later wrote about the nerve-wracking experience:

Bill [Stultz], of course, was at the controls. Slim [Gordon], gnawing a sandwich, sat beside him, when out of the mists there grew a blue shadow, in appearance no more solid than hundreds of other "land-

The New York Times.

"All the News That's Fit to Print."

THE WEATHER

VOL. LXXVII...No. 25,714   NEW YORK, TUESDAY, JUNE 19, 1928.   TWO CENTS

AMELIA EARHART FLIES ATLANTIC, FIRST WOMAN TO DO IT;
TELLS HER OWN STORY OF PERILOUS 21-HOUR TRIP TO WALES;
RADIO QUIT AND THEY FLEW BLIND OVER INVISIBLE OCEAN

RITCHIE WITHDRAWS IN FAVOR OF SMITH, URGING PARTY UNITY

NOBILE VAINLY HAILS FLIERS CIRCLING OVER BUT NOT SEEING HIM

FOUGHT RAIN, FOG AND SNOW ALL THE WAY

Miss Earhart Says Motors Spat and Gas Ran Low, But She Had Neither Fear Nor Doubt of Success.

PASSED OVER IRELAND WITHOUT EVEN SEEING IT

President of Porto Rican Senate Stabbed And Badly Hurt by a Maniac Anarchist

SMITH SUPPORTERS SEE A QUICK VICTORY

12 INJURED BY BOMB 'PLANTED' IN DETROIT

Eager Crowds Imperil Miss Earhart As They Welcome Fliers at Burry Port

FIRST WOMAN TO FLY THE ATLANTIC.

By AMELIA EARHART.

---

scapes" we had sighted before. ... It was land! I think Slim yelled. ... Bill permitted himself a smile.

The *Friendship* landed safely at Burry Port, Wales, and Earhart made history. She was now the first woman to successfully cross the Atlantic Ocean in an airplane.

The front page of the June 19, 1928, edition of The New York Times *heralded Earhart's historic accomplishment.*

7 FAME

Chapter

⤳⧟⤳

After her transatlantic adventure, Earhart received an avalanche of offers—from movie deals to marriage proposals. Fans flocked around her wherever she went, and she received countless letters of congratulations. Among them were notes from Mabel Boll, U.S. President Calvin Coolidge, and Ruth Elder, a woman who had failed in her own attempt to cross the Atlantic.

Although she declined the movie and marriage offers, Earhart knew fame was the price she would pay for the choice she had made. She dealt graciously with the attention and the fans. However, she was quick to give all the credit for the transatlantic flight to Stultz and Gordon. She made it clear she was only a passenger.

After Earhart's historic flight, she was congratulated by Lucia Marion Welch, the mayor of Southampton, England.

Ruth Elder was the first woman to attempt to fly from the United States to Europe. However, she wouldn't succeed. On October 11, 1927, along with pilot George Haldeman, Elder was forced by bad weather and a leaking oil line on her plane, the American Girl, to land on the ocean about 2,600 miles (4,160 km) into her transatlantic flight. They were only about 300 miles (480 km) from their goal. Elder and Haldeman were rescued by a Dutch ship. As the American Girl was being lifted out of the water, it caught on fire and was destroyed.

Not everyone was kind to Earhart. Some saw no value in what she'd accomplished and said so publicly. Some newspapers printed editorials that said she should have better ways to spend her time. Other reporters wrote stories that made Earhart sound unintelligent, not like the educated woman she really was. Instead of getting angry, Earhart took it all in stride.

On June 28, 1928, Earhart and the *Friendship* crew traveled back to the United States aboard the USS *President Roosevelt*. It was Earhart's first voyage on a ship and quite a learning experience for her. She quickly made friends with the ship's captain, Harry Manning. By watching him plot his course, Earhart learned a lot about navigation.

When the ship arrived in New York City, the mayor sent his yacht to pick up the adventurers. On land, convertible cars waited to drive Earhart and her crew to City Hall. A ticker tape parade and a variety of social events awaited them not only in New York but also in Boston, Chicago,

The crew of the Friendship was honored in New York City with a ticker tape parade.

and Medford, Massachusetts.

George Putnam was pleased with Earhart's accomplishment and had great plans for her. The year before, he had published Charles Lindbergh's book about his experience as the first person to fly across the Atlantic. Now he saw the tale of Earhart's historic journey as a best-selling story for his publishing house. Earhart agreed to write it. Putnam made arrangements for her to work at his home in Rye, New York, where she wouldn't be bothered. He also hired a secretary to help her. On an average day, Earhart received about 200 letters. She tried to personally answer all the ones sent by children. For those wanting autographs, she sent postcards or

George Putnam looked on as Earhart sat on a glider.

simply signed the original letter and sent it back.

She also flew whenever she found time. Before returning to the United States from her historic flight, she had purchased an Avro Avian airplane in England. Now, two months after her transatlantic journey, she began a cross-country vacation by air. During the first part of the journey, Putnam joined her. But when Earhart brought the plane down at Rodgers Field in Pittsburgh, Pennsylvania, it hit an unmarked ditch and nearly flipped over. Earhart and Putnam escaped without injury, but it wouldn't be their last mishap.

Earhart later had to land with a flat tire, and while traveling in Arizona, she was forced to land because of an overheated motor. She went on to her destination—Los Angeles—and back to New York, which made her the first woman to solo round-trip across North America.

In New York, Putnam scheduled a lecture tour so Earhart could promote her new book, *20 Hours, 40 Minutes: Our Flight in the Friendship.* People everywhere wanted to hear about her adventures. She spoke as many as 27 times a month but never complained. *Cosmopolitan* magazine hired her as an associate editor to write at least eight articles a year. The money she earned from speaking and writing helped pay for her flying.

In June 1929, Earhart's attention turned to her family. Her sister, Muriel, was getting married to

Albert Morrissey, and Earhart was the maid of honor. But by August, Earhart's thoughts were again on flying. She signed up for the first women's air race— the Women's Air Derby—that would start in California and end in Ohio. Earhart sold her Avian and bought a Lockheed Vega for the event. The plane was old and in poor shape, but she flew it anyway from New York to the Lockheed airplane factory in California to have it inspected. A Lockheed pilot was shocked that the rusty bucket could even fly. Lockheed officials were so impressed that Earhart had made the cross-country trip in the old Vega that they decided to give her a new plane.

Comedian Will Rogers was, among other things, a Wild West show performer, a trick roper, and host of air circuses and airplane races in the early 1920s.

Equipped with her brand new plane, Earhart joined 18 other women in Santa Monica, California, for the start of the race. Humorist and entertainer Will Rogers was the announcer. In his typical style of making fun, he noted that the pilots had to put one last dab of powder on their noses before the race began. Then he dubbed it the Powder Puff Derby. The women pilots took the race very seriously and found Rogers annoying.

The race wasn't easy. In Yuma, Arizona, Earhart's plane smashed into a sandbank while landing. She wasn't injured, but her plane wasn't so lucky. In a show of sportsmanship common among female pilots of that day, the other racers waited until Earhart's plane was fixed before continuing. Later, Earhart returned the courtesy when she stopped to help pilot Ruth Nichols get out of her damaged aircraft. Not all the pilots made it to the end of the race. Marvel Crosson was forced to jump from her plane. Unable to open her parachute, she plunged to her death. Some people wanted to stop the race, but the pilots voted unanimously to continue.

Born in 1879 in what would become Oklahoma, Will Rogers expressed great pride in his background, including his Cherokee Indian ancestry. Rogers grew up to become a well-known author, humorist, and radio and movie star. He appeared in more than 70 movies, including 50 silent films. He became famous for his homespun humor and practical attitude. Among his most famous lines is, "I never met a man I didn't like." Rogers died in a plane crash near Point Barrow, Alaska, in 1935.

Louise Thaden and Gladys O'Donnell took first and second places. Earhart placed third, but she wasn't disappointed. Winning was never important to her. She just wanted to show that women could be good pilots. By this time, there were about 60 licensed

Women pilots gathered at Clover Field in Santa Monica, California, in 1929, for the start of the first National Women's Air Derby. Amelia Earhart is the fourth pilot from the right.

female pilots in the United States. Many of them decided it was time to organize, and Earhart and Nichols encouraged others to help them form a women's pilot organization. Named for the number of charter members who formed the group, it was called the Ninety-Nines. Earhart was elected the first president.

Her world of flying was soon interrupted again with family matters. Earhart's father was dying of stomach cancer in California. Money was still a problem for him, so Earhart helped ease his worries by paying off the mortgage on his home. Muriel and her husband were also having financial difficulties. Earhart provided a $2,500 loan so they could buy a house in West Medford, Massachusetts. When Muriel became pregnant, Earhart sent her more money to make sure everyone in the household was well taken care of, including their mother, who lived with Muriel's family.

Earhart's attention also turned to Putnam. In December 1929, Putnam and his wife, Dorothy, divorced. Within hours, Earhart's phone was ringing. Reporters wanted to know if she would become the next Mrs. Putnam. She flatly denied any romance with him. In fact, she said she wasn't sure she would ever marry anyone.

In January 1930, after Dorothy remarried, Putnam proposed to Earhart. She politely turned him down. He would ask at least five more times that year, but each time Earhart would say no. She was still concentrating on flying.

On June 25, 1930, Earhart set two airspeed records. She pushed her Lockheed Vega to 174.89 miles (274.38 km) per hour over a 62½-mile (100-km) route. In another flight, she traveled the same distance, but this time her Vega carried a payload of 1,112 pounds (500 kilograms). She flew at 171.49 miles (274.38 km) per hour, a record with this load.

Lockheed donated a Lockheed Vega airplane to Earhart, who went on to set speed and pay-load records with it.

In the fall, Earhart returned to California to spend time with her terminally ill father and his second wife, Helen. On her way back to New York on September 23, 1930, Earhart received a telegram in Tucson, Arizona. Her father had died eight hours after she had left. Earhart flew back to California for the funeral.

But happier days were ahead. Putnam proposed again, and this time, 33-year-old Earhart said yes. The couple was married in a five-minute ceremony on February 7, 1931, at Noank, Connecticut. Six people were there—Earhart, Putnam, the judge, the judge's son, Putnam's mother, and Putnam's uncle. Earhart was dressed in what people had come to expect—brown.

Earhart's mother wasn't happy about the union. She disapproved because Putnam was divorced and nearly 10 years older than her daughter. Earhart still wasn't entirely sure about marriage, either. She made sure Putnam knew she needed her freedom, despite the fact that she was his wife. She made him promise that if things didn't work out after their first year of marriage, they would part. Putnam agreed, but their marriage remained strong, and they stayed together. Although married, Earhart continued to use her given name—Amelia Earhart—which was unusual for women of that time. 🐦

8 SOLO OVER THE ATLANTIC

❦

In April 1932, Earhart was playing a game of croquet with her husband and their friend, pilot Bernt Balchen, but she had other things on her mind. Suddenly, she bombarded Balchen with questions about the possibility of her flying solo across the Atlantic Ocean. "Am I ready to do it? Is the ship ready? Will you help me?" she asked him.

Her questions didn't surprise her husband. Earlier that year, Earhart had told him about her interest in this great adventure. She would be taking a risk; after all, 20 people had lost their lives trying to accomplish this feat in the past five years. Although Putnam had mixed feelings about the flight, he was proud of his wife's adventure and spirit. He said he would support her in whatever she chose to do.

Amelia Earhart and her husband George Putnam (1887–1950) in 1932

Earhart, Putnam, and Balchen took a break from their croquet game and discussed the idea. What Balchen had to say made Earhart's heart leap with joy. "Yes," he said. "You can do it. The ship [airplane]—when we are through with it—will be O.K. And—I'll help."

Balchen took Earhart's Vega to Teterboro Airport in New Jersey, where he and mechanic Eddie Gorski modified it for the transatlantic flight. Earhart kept her plans secret, even from her mother and Muriel. She also spent time in a simulator to perfect her skills at instrument flying.

Bernt Balchen encouraged Earhart to make a transatlantic flight.

On May 19, 1932, while Earhart was at Teterboro, Putnam called to tell her the weather was good enough to fly to Newfoundland, Canada. That was all the encouragement she needed, and she bounded into her car and drove back home to Rye, New York. She changed her clothes and grabbed her maps, toothbrush, comb, tomato juice, and a thermos for soup. By the time she got back to the New Jersey airport, her husband was waiting for her.

At 3 P.M., the Vega left New Jersey bound for St. John, New Brunswick, in Canada. Balchen flew the plane as Earhart and Gorski relaxed. Earhart would need all her energy for the flight across the Atlantic.

After spending the night at St. John, the crew flew to Harbour Grace in Newfoundland. After stopping at a restaurant to fill her thermos with tomato soup, Earhart boarded the Vega by herself, took her position at the controls, and headed over the Atlantic. She left just before 6 P.M. on May 20, 1932, exactly five years after Lindbergh had accomplished the same feat.

What had been predicted as a flight into clear night skies quickly turned into a nightmare. The skies around the Vega filled with fog. Earhart tried to climb above it, but the change in altitude meant a change in temperature, and moisture from the fog caused ice to form on the plane's wings. Earhart knew ice buildup could cause a deadly spin, so she reduced the plane's altitude and flew closer to the ocean.

Born in Norway in 1899, Colonel Bernt Balchen became one of the leading experts on the Arctic. On November 29, 1929, he piloted the first plane across the South Pole. He became a U.S. citizen in 1931 and was a hero during World War II. Among his many feats, Balchen led top-secret missions to Norway to take supplies to underground forces fighting the Germans who had overrun the country. As a veteran of the U.S. Air Force, Balchen continued to serve on special assignments and worked as a consultant for the aviation and energy industries until his death in 1973.

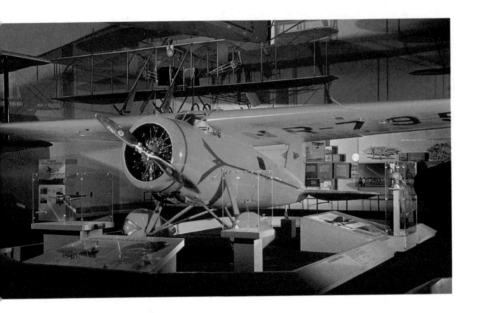

Earhart's refurbished Lockheed Vega is on display at the Smithsonian National Air and Space Museum in Washington, D.C.

Unfortunately, for the first time in Earhart's career, the altimeter, the instrument that shows how high the plane is in the air, quit working. From that moment, Earhart could not rely on her instruments. She had to find some balance between being high enough above the water and not so high that ice would form on the wings.

There were other problems, too. She had to fly through a lightning storm that lasted nearly an hour. "The gasoline gauge in the cockpit broke," she recalled, "and I was getting gas all down the back of my neck." To make matters worse, a small flame had formed around the exhaust manifold. Earhart prayed that the heavy metal would last the entire flight. She had no intention of giving up, but the problems did cause her to change her course. Instead of flying to Paris, France, as she had originally planned, she headed to Ireland.

Meanwhile, word of Earhart's solo flight leaked to the press. Reporters and those who loved her waited anxiously for word of her safe landing. Talk that she had crashed in France began to circulate, but it quickly proved to be untrue.

Nearly 15 hours after leaving North America, Earhart landed in a meadow in Culmore, near Londonderry, Northern Ireland. She taxied the Vega to a farmhouse owned by Robert Gallagher. The surprised farmer drove Earhart to Londonderry, where she could call her husband. An excited Irish crowd greeted her there. But after she made her call, Earhart returned with Gallagher to his farm and took him up on his offer to stay with his family. She wanted to be near her plane. Reporters quickly found the farm and swarmed around Earhart. She graciously answered their questions until she could no longer stay awake. After all, she hadn't slept since she left Newfoundland.

Putnam sailed to Europe on the USS *Olympic* to help Earhart deal with all the attention. She was still surprised at how famous she had become. Although she had flown across the Atlantic to fulfill a personal goal, to the world, it was an amazing feat. She received congratulatory messages from many

Well-wishers in Ireland greeted Earhart after her historic transatlantic flight.

people, including Lindbergh and President Herbert Hoover, who wrote:

> You have demonstrated not only your own dauntless courage, but also the capacity of women to match the skill of men in carrying through the most difficult feats of high adventure.

Everywhere Earhart went, people gathered in droves to catch a glimpse of her. In Great Britain, she was invited to banquets and receptions in her honor. The prince of Wales, who would later become King Edward VIII of England in 1936, extended an invitation to visit, which she accepted. Earhart also received the Certificate of Honorary Membership from the British Guild of Air Pilots and Navigators. She was only the second foreigner to be granted this high honor.

On June 3, 1932, Earhart traveled to France aboard the *Evadne*, a yacht owned by the president of the Royal Aeronautical Society. Then she traveled by train to Gare St. Lazare in Paris, where so many people were waiting on the tracks that the locomotive was forced to crawl to a halt about 50 feet (15 m) from its regular stop.

After her stay in France, Earhart visited Italy before heading back to the United States on the ship *Ile de France.* As she departed on June 15, three French planes dropped flowers onto the ship's deck as a farewell gesture.

In the United States, Earhart's welcome was just as sensational. Her successful adventure gave people something to celebrate. The country was in the midst of the Great Depression, a time of enormous economic hardship, and happy news was joyously welcomed. The American people celebrated

Earhart's accomplishments with ticker tape parades and almost constant social invitations. In a special ceremony on June 21, 1932, at Constitution Hall in Washington, D.C., President Hoover awarded Earhart the National Geographic Society's gold medal. She was the 16th recipient and the first woman to receive the distinguished award. As usual, Earhart was very humble and downplayed the significance of her accomplishment. She drew attention to Balchen for his help in making her wish come true.

That same day, the U.S. Congress awarded Earhart the Distinguished Flying Cross. Despite

President and Mrs. Hoover presented Earhart with the National Geographic Society's gold medal award in 1932.

these grand honors, perhaps none meant more than the honorary doctor of science degree awarded to her by Thiel College, where her father had attended.

Never one to sit still, Earhart soon went back to flying. She made a cross-country flight across the United States and continued to compete in flying derbies while she toured the country giving speeches. On December 17, 1933, she spoke at the new Benjamin Franklin Memorial and Franklin Institute Museum in Philadelphia, Pennsylvania, where the Vega she flew in her transatlantic flight was on exhibit. Among those in the audience was Orville Wright, the first person to experience flight in a heavier-than-air machine.

Now that both man and woman had conquered the Atlantic, Earhart set her sights on another ocean. This time, the vast Pacific loomed as a challenge to be conquered. The year 1934 was drawing to a close, and Earhart was planning her next big adventure.

Orville and Wilbur Wright became interested in flying while working at their bicycle shop in Dayton, Ohio. They began building gliders in 1899. In 1903, they built their first airplane, which they called the Flyer. *On December 17, 1903, near Kitty Hawk, North Carolina, Orville flew for 12 seconds, becoming the first person to fly in a machine that was heavier than air. Though few paid attention to the feat, the Wright brothers continued to improve their airplanes and became known as great pioneers of flight.*

9 BREAKING MORE NEW GROUND

Chapter

⤳⧉⤶

In December 1934, Earhart and Putnam sailed on the *Lurline* across the Pacific Ocean from California to Honolulu, Hawaii. With them were their friends Paul and Myrtle Mantz. Also onboard was Earhart's Vega.

Just a month before, Sir Charles Kingsford-Smith and Captain F.G. Taylor had become the first to fly from Hawaii to the United States. Now Earhart hoped to make the same flight. But she wanted to fly alone, which would make her the first person to fly solo over this expanse of the Pacific Ocean.

At first, the U.S. Navy refused to grant her clearance to fly. Naval officials claimed her radio didn't have enough range. But while Earhart was giving a speech at the University of Hawaii, Mantz took her Vega on a test flight to check the radio. His

Earhart was decorated with leis during her first visit to Honolulu, Hawaii.

radio transmission could be heard as far away as Seattle, Washington. The Navy reversed its decision and cleared Earhart's flight.

Heavy rain grounded the flight until January 11, 1935. Although more rain was predicted later that day, Earhart decided to fly. It was a relatively easy flight with no mechanical problems. When she landed at Oakland Airport in California, thousands of people waited to catch a glimpse of her. More rounds of speaking engagements and honors followed. On January 31, she traveled to the White House in Washington, D.C., to be congratulated by President Franklin D. Roosevelt and his wife, Eleanor. Earhart had come to know them when Roosevelt was elected president in 1932. In fact, once while Earhart and Eleanor were on a night flight over the city of Baltimore, Maryland, the two made plans for Eleanor to take flying lessons. Eleanor had already taken her physical examination to become a pilot when her husband put his foot down and told her no.

Franklin D. Roosevelt (1882–1945) was the 32nd president of the United States.

Amelia Earhart pointed out the White House to first lady Eleanor Roosevelt on a short flight from Baltimore, Maryland, in 1933.

On March 16, Earhart accepted an invitation from Mexican President Lazaro Cardenas to visit his homeland and be honored with a medal from the Mexico Society of Geography. When she arrived, the Mexican people treated her like a celebrity. On her flight back to the United States, Earhart set another record by flying nonstop from Mexico City to Newark, New Jersey. The only other attempt at this journey had ended in the death of the pilot when stormy conditions caused the plane to crash. Police couldn't hold back the crowd that waited to greet her at Newark Airport. Earhart recalled the incident:

In due course I was rescued from my plane by husky policemen, one of whom in the ensuing melee took possession of my right arm and another of my left leg. ... For the arm-holder started to go one way while he who clasped my leg set out in the opposite direction. The result provided the victim with a fleeting taste of the tortures of the rack.

She ended up walking under her own power to the New Jersey National Guard hangar.

Earhart continued her busy speaking schedule. In 1935 alone, she gave nearly 140 speeches. One woman was so touched by her speech that she wrote a note to Earhart's mother: "We all thought Lindbergh was a marvel but our 'Amelia' has shown the world what a woman can do." The press soon dubbed her "Lady Lindy" to compare her to Lindbergh, who had also crossed the Atlantic.

In September 1935, Earhart began working as a consultant in the department for the study of careers for women at Purdue University. The school also asked her to serve as technical adviser for the Department of Aeronautics. Purdue then established the Amelia Earhart Fund for Aeronautical Research. The fund grew to $80,000, and with it, Earhart bought a bigger and better plane—the Lockheed Electra 10E. The twin-engine aircraft was large enough to carry 10 passengers. It was Lockheed's first all-metal plane that

10 AROUND THE WORLD

⤙✦⤚

Amelia Earhart knew she couldn't fly around the world by herself. In the past, she'd flown alone to continents, which were easy to spot. But on her flight around the world, she planned one of her landings to be on tiny Howland Island about halfway between Hawaii and Australia. The island was only 2½ miles (4 km) long and ½ mile (.8 km) wide. A target that small could easily be missed, so Earhart knew she needed to bring along at least one navigator.

To Earhart, the choice was simple—Harry Manning, captain of the USS *President Roosevelt*, who had taught her so much about navigation. He agreed to serve as Earhart's navigator and took a six-month leave from his ship duties to work with her on the around-the-world flight. Also onboard would be technical adviser Paul

Pilot Amelia Earhart and her navigator, Fred Noonan, with a map of their planned around-the-world flight

Mantz and second navigator Fred Noonan.

Many other people worked to prepare for the 24,557-mile (39,291-km) journey. It took weeks to secure the maps and charts that the crew of the Electra would need. Earhart planned to fly as close to the equator as possible. This meant covering some territory that wasn't very well-mapped in 1937, so Earhart sought help from the expert navigators to plot her course.

The original crew of the around-the-world flight was Harry Manning (left), Amelia Earhart, Fred Noonan, and Paul Mantz.

Putnam made sure the Electra's crew of four had the proper visas and clearances to land and take off

at the various stops planned along the route. Others made sure fuel would be available at each landing. But not everyone was enthusiastic about her adventure. Some of Earhart's closest friends feared the journey was too dangerous and tried to talk her out of it. However, Earhart wouldn't be discouraged. She said:

> *I've wanted to do this flight for a long time. ... I've worked hard and I deserve one fling during my lifetime. If I should bop off, it will be doing the thing I've always wanted most to do. ... The Man with the little black book has a date marked down for all of us—when our work here is finished.*

Even her husband tried to change her mind. But Earhart told him:

> *Please don't be concerned. It just seems that I must try this flight. I've weighed it all carefully. With it behind me life will be fuller and richer. I can be content. Afterward it will be fun to grow old.*

During a February 11, 1937, press conference in New York City, Earhart officially announced her plan to fly around the world. She would fly west from Los Angeles, getting the difficult Pacific Ocean journey out of the way first.

On March 17, 1937, the crew left. They flew

On her first attempt to fly around the world, Earhart flew her Lockheed Electra 10E over the Golden Gate Bridge in San Francisco, California, on her way to Hawaii. The trip was later abandoned when the plane crashed on takeoff in Hawaii.

2,400 miles (3,840 km) from California to Hawaii, the first and longest leg of the journey, but now bad weather held them up. When the sky finally cleared enough for the plane to take off on March 20, the crew had been reduced to Earhart, Manning, and Noonan. Mantz had been removed over personal disagreements. As the plane began to taxi down the runway, it ground-looped, something like skidding in a car, and crashed. The crew was uninjured, but the Electra was severely damaged.

The plane had to be crated and returned by boat to the Lockheed factory in California for repairs.

Undaunted, Earhart said the flight would resume once the plane was fixed. Manning couldn't continue, however, since he had to get back to his ship. Noonan took over as sole navigator and now the only passenger. He and Earhart returned to California to await the repairs.

It took two months for Lockheed to fix the plane. Weather in the Caribbean and Africa was not so favorable now, so the course was changed. They would be flying east, so the most difficult leg of the journey—the long stretch from New Guinea to the tiny Howland Island—would now be near the end when Earhart and Noonan would be the most tired. But Earhart refused to give up on her dream.

On May 21, Earhart and Noonan flew unannounced from Burbank, California, to Miami, Florida, to test the plane. They quietly left the Miami airport on June 1, 1937, and soon after, the world learned their second attempt to fly around the world had begun.

Earhart and Noonan headed for Puerto Rico, the first leg of the trip. Newspapers carried stories on the progress of the flight. As they crossed the Amazon in Brazil, Earhart and Noonan enjoyed the beauty of the land and the cloud formations. Then the Electra flew to the coast of Africa and on to India and Indonesia. As the plane touched down in exotic places, Earhart vowed to come back again when she could spend more time enjoying the beautiful lands.

On June 29, the Electra landed in Lae, New Guinea. Only 5,962 miles (9,549 km) remained before Earhart and Noonan would be back in the United States. But the next stop was Howland Island, still 2,224 miles (3,558 km) away. Noonan knew the landing would be a challenge in the midst of the vast Pacific Ocean, but he was confident in his ability to find the island; his life and the life of his pilot depended on it.

Everything that could be removed from the Electra was taken out to allow for the weight of extra fuel and to give the plane maximum flying distance. The U.S. Coast Guard cutter *Itasca,* stationed off the shores of

Earhart's five historic flights

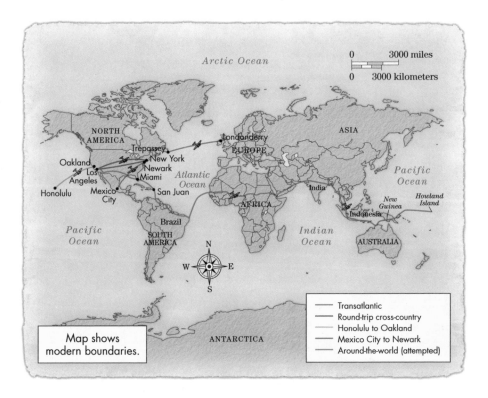

Howland Island, would guide the Electra using high-powered direction-finding equipment, if necessary.

Earhart left Lae around 10 A.M. on July 2, 1937. Despite favorable weather reports, the skies turned cloudy, and it rained occasionally. This posed a problem for Noonan, who used the position of the sun and stars to determine the plane's position. Radio communication wasn't good, and since neither Earhart nor Noonan knew Morse code very well, they couldn't communicate by telegraph. Besides, they had left their telegraph equipment in Miami.

Radio transmissions from the Electra to the ship were sporadic, faint, and often interrupted by static. At 7:42 A.M., Earhart's desperate voice was picked up at a high signal strength, which meant the plane must be close by: "We must be on you but cannot see you." Earhart added:

> *The largest ocean in the world, the Pacific covers nearly one-third of Earth's surface. The Pacific got its name from Portuguese explorer Ferdinand Magellan, the first European to sail across the Pacific Ocean in the early 1520s. Although pacific means peaceful, the Pacific Ocean often spawns hurricanes and typhoons. Earthquakes and volcanic eruptions can cause huge walls of water called tsunamis to form as well.*

Running out of gas. Only one half hour left. Been unable to reach you by radio. We are flying at one thousand feet.

*The cockpit
of Earhart's
Lockheed
Electra 10E*

The conversation was recorded in the *Itasca* log book, but it merely read, "Gas is running low."

About an hour later, the ship received another short transmission that provided some information on the plane's position. But it wasn't enough to locate the Electra. That radio transmission was the last. Earhart and Noonan were never heard from again. Neither their bodies nor the plane were found.

The story of the Electra's disappearance hit newspapers worldwide on July 3, 1937. A hopeful Putnam, in an interview with reporters in Oakland, California, said:

*The plane should float but I couldn't esti-
mate for how long, because a Lockheed
plane has never been forced down before.
The plane's large wing and empty gasoline tanks should provide sufficient buoy-
ancy if it came to rest on the sea without
being damaged.*

The search for Earhart's airplane was the largest rescue attempt ever made for a single lost plane. Sixty-six planes and 4,000 people on nine ships covered about 250,000 square miles (400,000 sq km) of the Pacific Ocean—an area about the size of Texas. The massive search lasted 16 days. On July 19, naval authorities ended their unsuccessful search.

Others, including Earhart's family, kept on searching. For years, Earhart's mother remained hopeful that her daughter would be found alive. Muriel said, "For two years Mother kept a suitcase packed with a few simple clothes, cold cream for sunburn and scissors to cut her hair in case Amelia were discovered on a tropical island."

Putnam spent money out of his own pocket to search for his wife. He chartered two small ships and paid the crews to search for Earhart and Noonan on and around Pacific islands near Howland. The searches proved fruitless. Although their bodies were never found, Fred Noonan was declared legally dead on June 26, 1938, and Amelia Earhart

Los Angeles Times

EQUAL RIGHTS

LIBERTY UNDER THE LAW   TRUE INDUSTRIAL FREEDOM

IN TWO PARTS — 34 PAGES

Part I — GENERAL NEWS — 18 Pages

TIMES OFFICES
202 West First Street
And Throughout Southern California

CC   SATURDAY MORNING, JULY 3, 1937.   DAILY, FIVE CENTS

Isolation of Paralysis Germ Told

Dr. E. C. Rosenow Discloses Epochal Research Here

Isolation of the germ which causes infantile paralysis, science's first major step in conquest of the dread disease, was announced last night in Glendale by Dr. Edward Carl Rosenow, professor of experimental bacteriology at the Mayo Foundation for Medical Education and Research at Rochester, Minn.

Addressing 300 physicians, surgeons and medical research workers at the Oakmont Country Club, Dr. Rosenow said that his work with saliva fluid taken from nurses who contracted the disease at the Los Angeles General Hospital in 1934 enabled him to isolate the micro-organism.

NEED OF SERUMS

Bits of muscle and swabs from the nose assisted in his work, Dr. Rosenow said.

Proof of isolation was obtained, he explained, when he injected the micro-organism into rabbits and later recovered it.

Asked what steps must be taken to fight the disease, now that isolation of the germ has been accomplished, Dr. Rosenow said that a serum must be developed, similar to serums used to combat ravages of other contagious ailments.

Already, the 62-year-old bacteriologist said, a composite vaccine has been prepared.

PRELIMINARY TESTS

"Preliminary tests indicate that favorable results should be forthcoming," he said. "It should be possible to immunize specifically and raise the resistance of patients and keep it at a high level and thus prevent recurrences."

Dr. Rosenow said that most important evidence of the streptococcal nature of the disease has been its reproduction in the essential respects.

"By the use of a small number of rabbits and mice, in three groups of experiments, we have produced the main symptoms of this disease as it now exists," he explained.

NINETEEN-YEAR STUDY

Dr. Rosenow has been studying infantile paralysis for nineteen years. His isolation of the germ was speeded by the epidemic at the General Hospital

Amelia Earhart Lost in Pacific; Radio Flashes Faint SOS

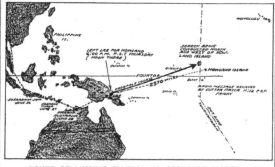

ROUTE OF MISSING FLYERS AND SCENE OF SEARCH

The probable course taken by Amelia Earhart and Navigator Frederick J. Noonan on their flight from Lae, New Guinea, to Howland Island, tiny sand spit in mid-Pacific, and the area in which their lost plane is being hunted by a Coast Guard cutter is shown by this map, drawn by Charles H. Owens, staff artist of The Times.

Revised Court Bill Submitted

Measure Given Senate Provides for Three Roosevelt Appointees

WASHINGTON, July 2. (P)—A Democratic substitute for the Roosevelt court bill went before the Senate today with an explanation by Senator Robinson, majority leader, that it would permit three appointments to the Supreme Court within the next six months.

FRANCE THREATENS TO AID LOYALISTS IN REBELLION

LONDON, July 2. (P)—Britain promptly rejected tonight a proposal of Italy and Germany that the naval patrol of Spanish coasts be abandoned and belligerent rights be accorded both parties in the Spanish civil war.

Backing up the refusal, France made clear tonight that she and Great Britain will supply arms, munitions and airplanes to the Spanish government unless Italy and Germany change their attitudes toward neutrality in Spain.

mean immediate reopening of the French frontier to the Spanish central government.

Insurgent Generalissimo Francisco Franco's frontier, it was said, would remain closed because he still would be viewed officially as the leader of an insurrection against Spain's legitimate government.

British rejection was considered to bring the whole European controversy over control to a stalemate. The subcommittee adjourned until next week, when

Miss Earhart's Signals Heard

Operators 'Unable to Tell Location of Plane in Pacific

Repeated radio calls of "SOS-KHAQQ" flashed across the Pacific Ocean last night indicating that Amelia Earhart and her 'round-the-world navigator, Capt. Fred Noonan, were still afloat at 1 a.m. today.

"SOS" was the international distress call and "KHAQQ" are

Plane Joins Ship Hunt for Flyers

Faint radio signals indicating that Amelia Earhart was still afloat somewhere in the vicinity of Howland Island at 1 a.m. today were picked up by Los Angeles radio amateurs and the British steamship Achilles. Repeated "SOS" calls followed by Miss Earhart's call letters "KHAQQ" were heard.

The Achilles was several hundred miles west of Miss Earhart's supposed position, too far to give her any quick assistance.

HONOLULU, July 3. (Saturday) (P)—Amelia Earhart, who started a world flight "just for fun," was lost today in the vast equatorial Pacific where sea and air searchers desperately sought her fuelless land plane which missed tiny Howland Island and plunged into the shark-infested ocean.

While the Coast Guard cutter Itasca sought aviation's first lady by sea, a Navy flying boat sped toward Howland Island on a 1532-mile flight to seek her by air. The Itasca was searching an area 100 miles northwest of Howland.

SHIP JOINS HUNT

The Navy minesweeper Swan joined the hunt from a position halfway between here and Howland, where it had been stationed to give any possible aid to Miss Earhart on the next leg of her flight.

The flying boat itself was undertaking a hazardous night

The July 3, 1937, edition of the Los Angeles Times *announced the disappearance of Earhart's airplane in the Pacific Ocean.*

on January 5, 1939.

Through the years, people have wondered what happened to Amelia Earhart. Did her plane run out of gas? Did she drown at sea? Did she reach land somewhere in the vast Pacific and die without anyone knowing it? Did she fly into Japanese territory? Was she captured and imprisoned? Researchers continued to investigate these questions. They have studied every known aspect of Earhart's ill-fated flight with the hope of solving the greatest aviation mystery of all time. They do so to honor one of the world's most courageous and fascinating women. They look forward to the day when her body and her airplane will be found and brought home.

What isn't a mystery, though, is what Amelia Earhart accomplished during her lifetime. A July 1937 editorial in *The New York Times* helped capture what people will always remember about this legendary aviator:

> One remembers the outward symbols of what she was—the slender hands and wrists ...; the voice that was soft and beautiful; the rich inflections, the animation that would have made her an actress; the feminine dignity that melted into humor. ... Perhaps in the vividness of her last glimpse of sun and sky and the curling tops of waves she knew that she had helped to make all women less afraid.

In 1997, 60 years after Earhart's disappearance, Linda Finch, Texas pilot and businesswoman, flew around the world on nearly the same flight path Earhart took in 1937. Others had flown that route, but Finch did it in a Lockheed Electra 10E, the same make and model as Earhart's plane. On March 17, 1997, Finch and a navigator took off from Oakland, California, and landed back there on May 28. The journey was called World Flight 1997.

EARHART'S LIFE

1907
Sees her first airplane at the Iowa State Fair

1905
Lives temporarily with maternal grandparents

1897
Born July 24 in Atchison, Kansas

1900

1898
The Spanish-American War gains Cuba its independence; Spain cedes the Philippines, Guam, and Puerto Rico to the United States for $20 million

1906
Earthquake and fires destroy most of San Francisco; more than 3,000 people die

WORLD EVENTS

1916

Graduates from Hyde
Park High School
and starts college at
Ogontz School

1918

Works at the Spadina
Military Hospital in
Toronto, Ontario

1919

Enrolls as a pre-
med student at
Columbia Univer-
sity in New York

1916

German-born physi-
cist Albert Einstein
publishes his general
theory of relativity

1919

The Treaty of
Versailles officially
ends World War I

EARHART'S LIFE

1921

Takes first flying lesson January 3; solos for the first time in June

1920

Rides in an airplane for the first time

1922

Buys her first plane on her 25th birthday

1920

1920

American women get the right to vote

1922

The tomb of Tutankhamen is discovered by British archaeologist Howard Carter

WORLD EVENTS

1928

Becomes the first
woman to fly
across the Atlantic

1930

Sets two airspeed
records

1926

Takes a job at
Denison House
in Boston

1930

1926

A.A. Milne publishes
Winnie the Pooh

1927

Charles Lindbergh
makes the first
solo nonstop
transatlantic flight
from New York
to Paris

1930

Clyde Tombaugh
discovers Pluto; he
was 24 years old

EARHART'S LIFE

1935
Becomes first person
to fly solo from
Hawaii to California

1932
Becomes first woman to
fly solo across the Atlantic;
wins National Geographic
Society's gold medal;
awarded Distinguished
Flying Cross

1931
Marries George
Putnam on
February 7

1935

1933
Nazi leader Adolf
Hitler is named chan-
cellor of Germany

1935
Persia is
renamed Iran

WORLD EVENTS

1936

Amelia Earhart Fund for Aeronautical Research established at Purdue University, where she works

1937

Begins around-the-world flight in March; disappears on the way to Howland Island July 2

1939

Declared legally dead January 5

1940

1936

African-American athlete Jesse Owens wins four gold medals at the Olympic Games in Berlin in the face of Nazi racial discrimination

1937

The German airship *Hindenburg* bursts into flames when attempting to land in Lakehurst, New Jersey

1939

German troops invade Poland; Britain and France declare war on Germany; World War II (1939–1945) begins

DATE OF BIRTH: July 24, 1897

BIRTHPLACE: Atchison, Kansas

FATHER: Edwin Stanton Earhart

MOTHER: Amy Otis Earhart

EDUCATION: Hyde Park High School, Chicago, Illinois; Ogontz School, Rydal, Pennsylvania; Columbia University, New York; Harvard University, Cambridge, Massachusetts

SPOUSE: George Putnam (1887–1950)

DATE OF MARRIAGE: February 7, 1931

DATE OF DEATH: Unknown; declared legally dead January 5, 1939

PLACE OF BURIAL: Her remains were never found

FURTHER READING

Jerome, Kate Boehm. *Who Was Amelia Earhart?* New York: Grosset & Dunlap, 2002.

Netzley, Patricia D. *The Disappearance of Amelia Earhart.* San Diego: Lucent Books, 2004.

Pflueger, Lynda. *Amelia Earhart: Legend of Flight.* Berkeley Heights, N.J.: Enslow Publishers, 2003.

Wagner, Heather Lehr. *Amelia Earhart.* Philadelphia: Chelsea House, 2003.

LOOK FOR MORE SIGNATURE LIVES
BOOKS ABOUT THIS ERA:

Thomas Alva Edison: *Great American Inventor*
ISBN 0-7565-1880-6

Langston Hughes: *The Voice of Harlem*
ISBN 0-7565-0993-9

Wilma Mankiller: *Chief of the Cherokee Nation*
ISBN 0-7565-1600-5

J. Pierpont Morgan: *Industrialist and Financier*
ISBN 0-7565-1890-3

Eleanor Roosevelt: *First Lady of the World*
ISBN 0-7565-0992-0

Franklin Delano Roosevelt: *The New Deal President*
ISBN 0-7565-1586-6

Elizabeth Cady Stanton: *Social Reformer*
ISBN 0-7565-0990-4

Gloria Steinem: *Champion of Women's Rights*
ISBN 0-7565-1587-4

Amy Tan: *Writer and Storyteller*
ISBN 0-7565-1876-8

Booker T. Washington: *Innovative Educator*
ISBN 0-7565-1881-4

On the Web

For more information on *Amelia Earhart,* use FactHound.

1. Go to *www.facthound.com*
2. Type in this book ID: 0756518806
3. Click on the *Fetch It* button.

FactHound will find the best Web sites for you.

Historic Sites

Amelia Earhart Birthplace Museum
223 N. Terrace St.
Atchison, KS 66002
913/367-4217
The home where Amelia Earhart was born

The National Women's Hall of Fame
76 Fall St.
Seneca Falls, NY 13148
315/568-8060
Exhibits and artifacts of Amelia Earhart and other great women in the history of the United States

aces
top fighter pilots

altimeter
an instrument that measures how high an airplane
is above sea level

altitude
the height of something above sea level or
Earth's surface

biplane
an airplane with two sets of wings, one above the
other, flown in the early 1900s

hangar
a large building in which aircraft are kept

manifold
a pipe with an opening for expelling engine gas

navigation
the science of plotting and following a course
from one place to another

payload
weight of cargo carried by a plane or other vehicle

retractable
able to be drawn in from an extended position

simulator
a device designed to reproduce what actually
occurs in reality

solo
carried out by one person alone

ticker tape
long narrow strips of paper on which stock prices
are printed; sometimes used during celebrations

Chapter 1

Page 9, line 6: Muriel Earhart Morrissey and Carol L. Osborne. *Amelia, My Courageous Sister*. Santa Clara, Calif.: Osborne Publisher, 1987, p. 86.

Page 9, line 12: Ibid.

Page 11, line 1: Donald M. Goldstein and Katherine V. Dillon. *Amelia: The Centennial Biography of an Aviation Pioneer*. Washington, D.C.: Brassey's, 1997, p. 55.

Page 13, line 6: Ibid., p. 54.

Page 13, line 18: Susan Butler. *East to Dawn: The Life of Amelia Earhart*. Reading, Mass.: Addison-Wesley, 1997, p. 192.

Chapter 2

Page 17, line 6: *Amelia, My Courageous Sister*, p. 16.

Page 18, line 10: Doris L. Rich. *Amelia Earhart: A Biography*. Washington, D.C.: The Smithsonian Institution, 1989, p. 4.

Page 19, line 8: *East to Dawn: The Life of Amelia Earhart*, p. 35.

Chapter 3

Page 26, line 25: *Amelia: The Centennial Biography of an Aviation Pioneer*, p. 20.

Chapter 4

Page 30, line 26: *Amelia: The Centennial Biography of an Aviation Pioneer*, p. 26.

Page 31, line 9: *East to Dawn: The Life of Amelia Earhart*, p. 85.

Page 32, line 3: Ibid.

Page 34, line 21: *Amelia: The Centennial Biography of an Aviation Pioneer*, p. 30.

Page 35, line 4: Ibid., p. 31.

Chapter 5

Page 37, line 13: Ibid.

Chapter 6

Page 45, line 10: Ibid., p. 39.

Page 48, line 1: *Amelia Earhart: A Biography*, p. 55.

Page 48, line 18: *East to Dawn: The Life of Amelia Earhart*, p. 170.

Page 48, line 23: Ibid.

Page 49, line 1: *Amelia Earhart: A Biography*, p. 56.

Page 52, line 15: *East to Dawn: The Life of Amelia Earhart*, p. 192.

Page 54, line 24: *Amelia: The Centennial Biography of an Aviation Pioneer*, p. 53.

Chapter 8

Page 69, line 6: Ibid., p. 94.

Page 70, line 4: Ibid.

Page 72, line 10: Ibid., p. 96.

Page 74, line 3: Ibid., p. 99.

Chapter 9

Page 82, line 1: Ibid., p. 140.

Page 82, line 15: *Amelia Earhart: A Biography*, p. 201.

Chapter 10

Page 87, line 7: *Amelia: The Centennial Biography of an Aviation Pioneer*, p. 162.

Page 87, line 16: Ibid., p. 165.

Page 91, line 23: Ibid., p. 234.

Page 91, line 25: Ibid.

Page 92, line 2: *Amelia, My Courageous Sister*, p. 243.

Page 93, line 1: *Amelia: The Centennial Biography of an Aviation Pioneer*, p. 241.

Page 93, line 18: Ibid., p. 261.

Page 95, line 17: Ibid., p. 257.

Select Bibliography

Butler, Susan. *East to Dawn: The Life of Amelia Earhart.* Reading, Mass.: Addison-Wesley, 1997.

Goldstein, Donald M., and Katherine V. Dillon. *Amelia: The Centennial Biography of an Aviation Pioneer.* Washington, D.C.: Brassey's, 1997.

Long, Elgen M. *Amelia Earhart: The Mystery Solved.* New York: Simon & Schuster, 1999.

Morrissey, Muriel Earhart, and Carol L. Osborne. *Amelia, My Courageous Sister.* Santa Clara, Calif.: Osborne Publisher, 1987.

Naval Historical Center. www.history.navy.mil/faqs/faq3-1.htm

Nichols, Ruth. *Wings for Life.* Philadelphia: J.B. Lippincott Company, 1957.

Purdue University Archives and Special Collections, www.lib.purdue.edu/spcol/aearhart/index.html

Rich, Doris L. *Amelia Earhart: A Biography.* Washington, D.C.: The Smithsonian Institution, 1989.

Brenda Haugen started in the newspaper business and had a career as an award-winning journalist before finding her niche as an author. Since then, she has written and edited many books, most of them for children. A graduate of the University of North Dakota in Grand Forks, Brenda lives in North Dakota with her family.

Image Credits

Photo provided courtesy of Purdue University, from Purdue University Libraries' The George Palmer Putnam Collection of Amelia Earhart Papers, cover (top), 4–5, 11, 18, 22, 36, 39, 60, 98 (top), 99 (top), 100 (top left); Hulton Archive/Getty Images, cover (bottom), 2, 31, 32, 78, 100 (top right); Bettmann/Corbis, 8, 12, 14, 43, 46, 49, 62, 70, 81, 84, 86, 96 (top); Corbis, 17, 76, 100 (top center); Minnesota Historical Society, 25; Chicago Historical Society image number DN-0059437/Chicago Daily, 27, 97 (left); Toronto Public Library, 28, 97 (middle); Smithsonian National Air and Space Museum, 35, 72; Library of Congress, 40, 92, 96 (bottom), 97 (right and bottom), 98 (bottom), 99 (bottom), 100 (bottom), 101 (bottom); E.O. Hoppé/Corbis, 41; Topical Press Agency/Getty Images, 44; J. Gaiger/Topical Press Agency/Getty Images, 47; Hulton-Deutsch Collection/Corbis, 50; Underwood & Underwood/Corbis, 53, 59, 64, 66; The Granger Collection, New York, 55, 74, 94, 101 (top); Keystone/Getty Images, 56; New York Times Co./Getty Images, 68; Stock Montage/Getty Images, 80; Keystone/Hulton Archive/Getty Images, 88.